OCEAN ESCAPE
COLORING BOOK

ARROLYNN WEIDERHOLD

DESIGN ORIGINALS
an Imprint of Fox Chapel Publishing
www.d-originals.com

It's Time to Start Coloring!

We're so glad you've picked up this coloring book, because we know you're going to find exactly what you're looking for here! Whether you're an experienced colorist or a beginner, whether you want to calm your mind or unleash your creativity, whether you just want to color or go crazy with crafting, this book has you covered, and here's why!

Need some advice? No problem! If you're a beginner, you'll learn everything you need to know to get started, from supplies to colorful inspiration. If you'd like a little help, we've provided guided coloring pages in the center of the book that start you off with a suggested color palette, finished example, and encouraging words. There's no need to feel intimidated!

Feeling creative? If you're looking for something new, check out our patterning and coloring techniques. Learn all about tangling and pumping up your pages with shading and blending. If you're feeling crafty, take a look at our ideas for craft projects incorporating colored pages.

Need to unwind? We get it! Every single page in this book was developed and hand-drawn by the author to give you the maximum benefits possible from coloring the images. By working with these designs, we know you are going to become relaxed, energized, and focused!

We know this book is going to give you exactly what you need: a little relaxation, some crafty ideas, and loads of coloring. What are you waiting for? It's time to get started!

MEET ARROLYNN

A Florida native, Arrolynn Weiderhold received a B.F.A. in Illustration from Ringling College of Art and Design and currently resides in Washington D.C., where she spends her time sketching at the zoo, museums, parks, and cafés. She draws inspiration from her collections of children's books, greeting cards, fabrics, and anything else she can get her hands on.

Frame your designs for beautiful home accents.

ISBN 978-1-4972-0233-7

This edition created especially for Michaels Stores by New Design Originals, an imprint of Fox Chapel Publishing.

Fox Chapel focuses on providing real value to our customers through the printing and book production process. We strive to select quality paper that is also eco-friendly. This book is printed on archival-quality, acid-free paper that can be expected to last for at least 200 years. It meets the minimum requirements of the American National Standard for Information Sciences—Permanence of Paper for Printed Library Materials, ANSI/NISO Z39.48-1992. This book is printed on paper produced from trees harvested from well-managed forests where measures are taken to protect wildlife, plants, and water quality.

Fair trade principles should also be recognized when dealing with the creative and artistic community. We are pleased that our business practices and payments to authors meet the criteria to display **DO Magazine's Fair Trade Seal of Approval**. In order to earn the seal, all of the artwork must be original (not clip art or public domain material); the author must be paid on a royalty basis at fair trade rates (not piecemeal or via flat rates), meaning the author participates financially in the success of his or her titles; and the work of contributing artists must be acknowledged in print. DO Magazine: Color, Tangle, Craft, Doodle, www.domagazines.com.

© 2016 by Arrolynn Weiderhold/Artlicensing.com and New Design Originals Corporation, www.d-originals.com, an imprint of Fox Chapel Publishing, 800-457-9112, 1970 Broad Street, East Petersburg, PA 17520.

Printed in the United States of America
First printing

Cover art colored by Kati Erney and Llara Pazdan. Back cover art colored by Arrolynn Weiderhold.
Craft projects and guided pages colored by Laura Brumby (p. 2), Nadena Gibson (p. 67), Ninna Hellman (p. 9 top right, p. 73), Annie Jump (p. 9 bottom right), Katja Lahti (p. 3 coaster), Lynette Parmenter (p. 79), Darla Tjelmeland (p. 3 bag, p. 9 middle left, p. 69), Arrolynn Weiderhold (p. 3 journal, p. 5 journal, p. 8, p. 9 top left and bottom left, p. 65, p. 71, p. 75, p. 77).

The Benefits of Coloring

A quick Internet search on this topic will yield pages of articles with statistics and opinions from the scientific research and art therapy communities. If you want to learn all about the science behind the benefits of coloring, we recommend you check them out. In the meantime, here are some of our favorite reasons for picking up the colored pencils.

Coloring allows for personal and creative expression. When it comes to coloring and creativity, there is no right or wrong. It's all about expressing your creativity your way. There are no limits to what you can do and no judgment (you don't have to show your coloring to someone else if you don't want to). The creativity of coloring provides a break from daily routine and can even make us more creative in other areas of our lives, like at work.

Colored designs can be decoupaged onto countless surfaces to make unique home dec pieces, like these coasters.

Coloring allows us to unplug. Coloring is totally screen free. It's just us, our supplies, and our creativity. Unplugging every once in a while is a great way to relax, focus, and recharge, so unplugging by coloring is doubly effective!

Coloring reduces stress and anxiety. Why? It's easy and therefore stress free. Even better, research shows that coloring actually relaxes the fear center of the brain, reducing stress and anxiety in the present, and improving the way we respond to stressful situations in the future!

Coloring brings about a meditative state. Coloring requires some focus, but not extreme concentration. By occupying part of the brain with the simple, repetitive act of coloring, the rest of the mind is free to let go and relax, switch off other thoughts, and focus on the present moment.

Coloring connects both sides of your brain. Coloring requires the logical, analytical side of your brain when choosing where colors go and filling in spaces in a design. It requires the imaginative side of your brain when selecting a color palette and making creative choices about patterning, shading, and blending. Doing these things together strengthens the connection between your right brain and left brain and also exercises your fine motor skills and vision.

Use your finished pieces to add a personal touch to cards, journals, and scrapbooks.

Transfer your colored designs onto fabric for custom bags, shirts, and more!

Coloring Supplies

As adult coloring grows in popularity, so has the variety of coloring supplies available. So, how do you choose? For coloring (and art in general), experimentation is the name of the game. What works well and feels comfortable for someone else might not work for you. When starting out, try a little bit of everything to get a feel for what you like and refine your choices from there. And remember, coloring is supposed to be fun and stress free. Don't get hung up on using the "right" marker. If you want some guidance, here are some things to consider when choosing coloring supplies.

Markers

If you like bright, saturated colors and quick results, you'll probably be drawn to markers. Markers yield vibrant colors and can cover a lot of ground quickly. For coloring, tip shape is an important consideration. Lots of adult coloring pages are intricate and have many small spaces. You want markers with points that will allow you to get into those tiny areas with precision. Markers with brush tips are very versatile, allowing you to color large spaces quickly while still being able to fill in small spaces. Even better, some markers are dual ended, with a brush tip at one end and a fine point at the other. Markers with bullet or chisel tips will make precision work tricky, but you can pair them with fine-tip pens in the same color—use the markers for large areas and the corresponding pens for detail work.

When it comes to markers, you will hear a lot of talk about alcohol- vs. water-based options. This refers to the contents of the marker—dye mixed with water or dye mixed with alcohol. If you're just getting started, you might be drawn to the more budget-friendly, water-based markers. As you grow more serious about coloring, you might be drawn to alcohol-based markers, which are built to last, often refillable, and are less prone to streaking, but they also come with a high price tag.

One great thing about professional-grade markers is that they are usually available for purchase individually. To experiment, try purchasing an inexpensive set of brush markers and one or two professional water-based and alcohol-based options. See which ones you like working with the most.

Colored Pencils

If you love adding depth and dimension to a colored design with shading and blending, colored pencils are the perfect fit for you. While high-quality markers *can* be layered and blended, colored pencils were *made* for this.

When purchasing colored pencils, point strength is an important consideration. This refers to how hard or soft the pigment within the pencil is. If you want to do lots of layering and blending, you'll appreciate pencils with soft point strength. These will provide a creamy application and cover large areas easily, but they will not hold a sharp point for long, so you'll have to do a fair amount of sharpening for detail work. If you want pencils that will get into all of the tiny spaces on your coloring page, you'll like pencils with hard point strength. These will stay sharper longer, giving you the best precision, but they will be more difficult to blend.

As you grow more serious about coloring, you might be looking for ways to create unique effects. Watercolor pencils give your piece a painted watercolor look without the need for painting expertise. You apply color with the pencils and then add water to create the painted effect. If you just want to color, though, regular colored pencils are all you need.

Like markers, colored pencils come at a variety of price points. To experiment, try purchasing an inexpensive student-grade set along with a few individual options at a higher price point. Purchase a variety of point strengths—soft, medium, and hard—to determine your preference.

Pens

If you love adding special touches to your coloring, pens are for you. With their fine points, regular colored pens can be used to color tiny spaces that your markers cannot get into, while paint pens and gel pens can be used to add patterning and accents on top of a piece that's already been colored.

If you really enjoy patterning, try purchasing one or two felt-tip pens to add doodles and details to a coloring page. You can pattern a design before coloring, or add the patterning to open areas like the background after coloring.

For special effects and accents, gel pens and paint pens are the way to go. Because their ink is opaque, these pens can be used to accent areas on pieces already colored with markers or colored pencils. Beyond that, you can purchase gel pens and paint pens in endless varieties, including metallic, sparkle, and neon, even glow in the dark! If you're not sure about the power of pens, purchase a white gel pen or paint pen and try using it to add accents to a colored design. We're sure you'll be back at the craft store looking for more!

Coloring Techniques

There are so many cool things you can do with a coloring page besides coloring it. You can make the design your own by adding patterning and flourishes, or you can add depth and dimension through shading and blending. Here are some techniques to try.

Patterning

Patterning might sound intimidating, but a pattern is really just a combination of basic shapes (like circles, lines, and triangles) that is repeated. And we can all draw triangles and circles, right? So we can definitely draw patterns. Here are some simple patterns for you to try.

Lines. It doesn't get any easier! Draw them with even spacing, close together, far apart, or all three! Try drawing curved lines or lines that crisscross.

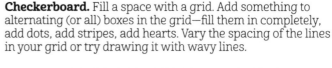

Checkerboard. Fill a space with a grid. Add something to alternating (or all) boxes in the grid—fill them in completely, add dots, add stripes, add hearts. Vary the spacing of the lines in your grid or try drawing it with wavy lines.

Circles. Draw them open or fill them in as dots. Make them all the same size or make some big and some small (like bubbles). Draw them in orderly rows or overlap them like ripples.

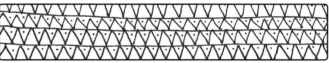

Triangles. Try adding triangles along a line on your coloring page. This is a really cool effect in and of itself, but you can take it further by adding dots or lines between the triangles or overlapping the triangles.

Need some help?

The Zentangle® method is a meditative drawing technique that uses simple, step-by-step patterns called tangles to produce unique art pieces. There are hundreds of tangles available online, a perfect resource for pattern ideas or step-by-step instructions. Try one of the tangles below on your next coloring page. To learn more about the Zentangle method, check out *Joy of Zentangle* or *Zentangle Basics, Expanded Workbook Edition* or connect with a Certified Zentangle Teacher (CZT) in your area (*www.zentangle.com*).

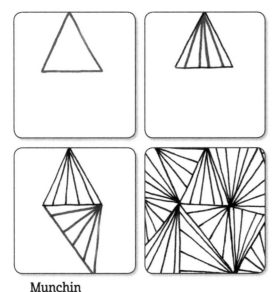

Munchin
An original Zentangle design

Flying Geese
Tangle by Suzanne McNeill, CZT

Shading and Blending

Shading and blending are wonderful ways to make a coloring page look more realistic, and they don't require a lot of expertise. Shading uses tints and shades of one color to add dimension. Blending uses multiple colors together to create cool gradations. Here are some simple ways to use shading and blending to make a design jump right off the page.

Go around the edges. Shading around the edge of a shape will add dimension. This can be done around a large shape, or around smaller areas within a shape. For example, you could shade around the entire flower (left) or just around the center circle (right).

Work from end to end. Try giving a shape dimension by working from a dark shade at one end to a light shade at the other end. The leaf at right is colored with three shades of green. To re-create this effect, select three shades of the same color: light, medium, and dark. Color the entire shape with the light color. Then, starting at one end, color two-thirds of the shape with the medium color. Then, starting at the same end, color one-third of the shape with the dark color. Go over the entire shape with the light color to help smooth the transitions between the shades.

Work from inside out or outside in. The same technique used to shade a shape from end to end can be used to shade a shape from the inside out (left) or the outside in (right).

Blend instead of shade. Blending follows the same steps as shading except it uses multiple colors instead of tints and shades of one color. For blending, you'll want a starting color, one or two transition colors, and a finishing color. For example, to blend from yellow to red, you'll want yellow (starting color), light orange (transition color), dark orange (transition color), and red (finishing color). Since you're working with four colors, mentally divide the shape you're working on into quarters. Color the entire shape yellow. Starting at one end, color three-quarters of the shape light orange. Starting at the same end, color half of the shape dark orange. Starting at the same end, color one-quarter of the shape red. Go over the entire shape with yellow to smooth over the transitions.

Gallery Wall

What better way to display your colored designs than by transforming them into a gallery wall feature! Here are some tips and tricks for creating a stunning gallery wall.

Map it out. How many frames do you want and in what size? Do you want an orderly grid pattern or a creative, eclectic layout? Will your frames be the same size, or will you enlarge or shrink some of your designs to fit frames of different sizes? Try out your design by cutting different frame sizes out of newspaper and hanging them on your wall to see if you like the look.

Pick your designs. Will you use only coloring pages or include some other pieces? What do you want to feature: your favorite designs, designs that are thematically similar, or designs with complementary color palettes?

Craft it up. If you're feeling extra crafty, try transferring one of your designs to wood or canvas. Experiment with color mats, or try cutting out small designs and attaching them to colorful paper for a pop of color in the background.

Pick your frames. Will all of your frames be exactly the same, or perhaps different styles but all in the same color? Maybe you want to mix and match black and white or choose bright, modern colors. Do you want frames with or without mats or a mix of both?

Hang it up. When all of your pieces are crafted and framed, it's time to hang them up using your chosen layout!

A Personal Touch

Coloring pages are a great way to add a personal touch to your home, your crafts, and even your gift giving. Check out the reverse side of each coloring page for a space designed for your creativity. Use it as a journaling page or a place to record notes about your coloring mediums and techniques. The page is made to be folded in three so you can mail your coloring page with a personal note if you're giving it as a gift.

Color by Arrolynn Weiderhold. *Colored pencils*

Color by Laura Brumby. *Colored pencils*

Color by Arrolynn Weiderhold. *Colored pencils*

Color by Katja Lahti. *Markers, fine-tip markers, colored pencils*

Color by Darla Tjelmeland. *Markers, colored pencils*

Color by Ninna Hellman. *Markers, colored pencils*

Color by Annie Jump. *Colored pencils, watercolor pencils*

On the beach, you can live in bliss.

—Dennis Wilson

Date

Name

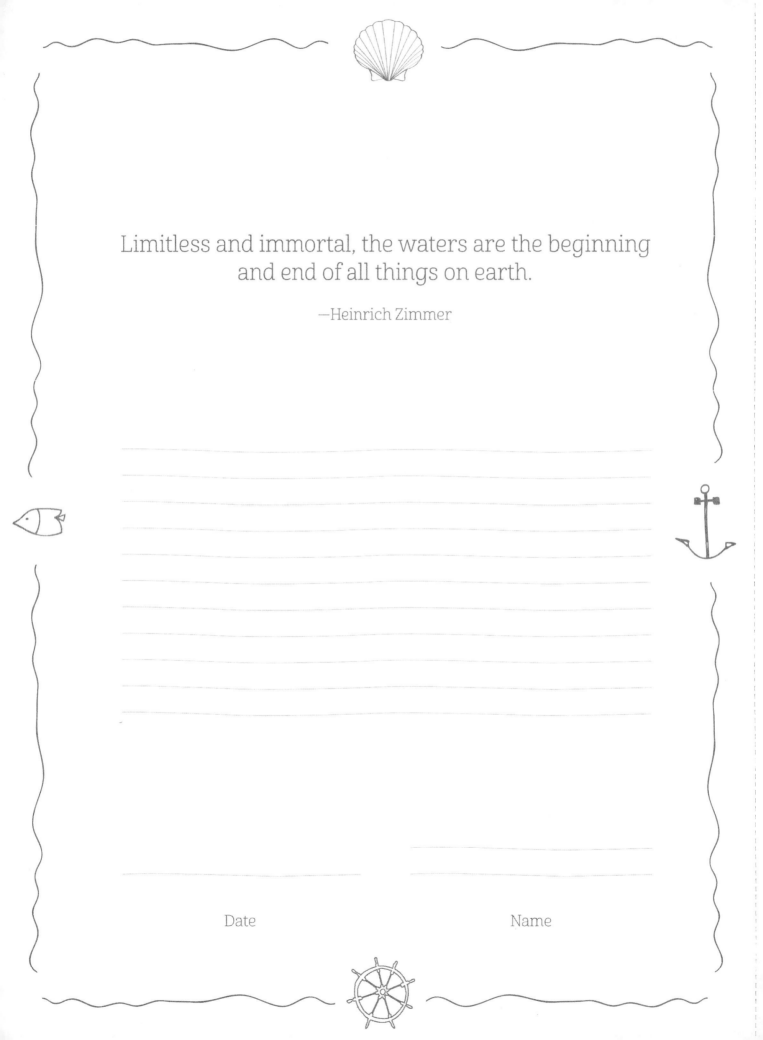

Limitless and immortal, the waters are the beginning
and end of all things on earth.

—Heinrich Zimmer

Date

Name

To young men contemplating a voyage
I would say go.

—Joshua Slocum

Date   Name

Sunshine is my favorite accessory.

—Unknown

Date   Name

The sea, once it casts its spell,
holds one in its net of wonder forever.

—Jacques Cousteau

Date   Name

Every time I slip into the ocean,
it's like going home.

—Sylvia Earle

Date   Name

If you cannot change the course of a storm,
be the lighthouse.

—Ronn Daigle

_____

_____

_____

_____

_____

_____

_____

_____

_____

_____

Date   Name

You can shake the sand from your shoes
but it never leaves your soul.

—Unknown

Date

Name

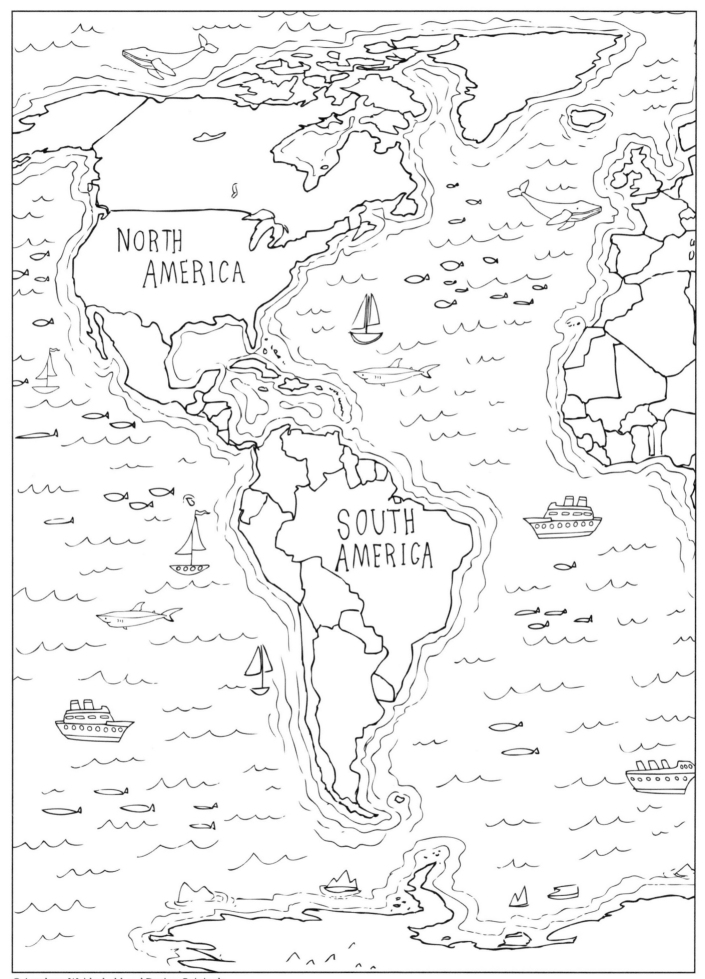

I cannot not sail.

—E. B. White, *The Sea and the Wind that Blows*

Date

Name

Now, voyager, sail thou forth, to seek and find.

—Walt Whitman, *The Untold Want*

Date   Name

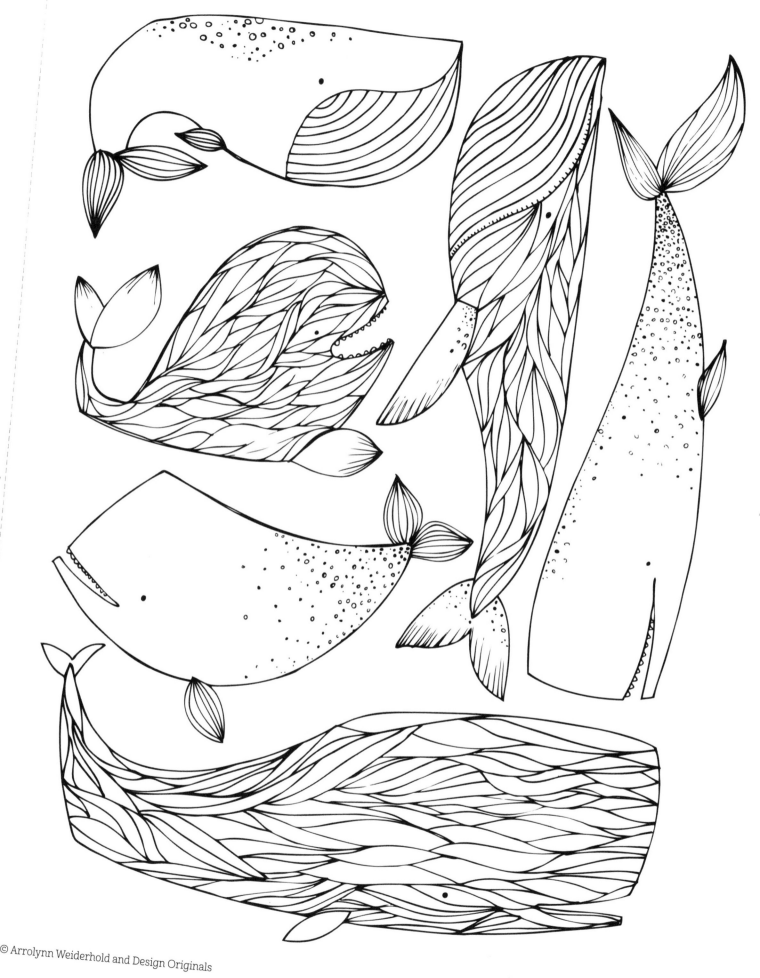

The world's finest wilderness lies beneath the waves.

—Wyland

Date   Name

I want to run the beach's length,
because it never ends.

—Deborah Ager

Date   Name

There comes a time in life when there is nothing else to do but to go your own way. A time to follow your dreams. A time to raise the sails of your own beliefs.

—Sergio Bambaren, *The Dolphin: Story of a Dreamer*

Date   Name

However bad the storm you are in, there is still sun somewhere over your horizon.

—Unknown

Date   Name

The ocean stirs the heart, inspires the imagination,
and brings eternal joy to the soul.

—Wyland

_____

Date   Name

You can't stop the waves, but you can learn to surf.

—Jon Kabat-Zinn

Date   Name

Because there's nothing more beautiful than the way the ocean refuses to stop kissing the shoreline, no matter how many times it's sent away.

—Sarah Kay

Date   Name

I want to be like water.
I want to slip through fingers, but hold up a ship.

—Michelle Williams

Date

Name

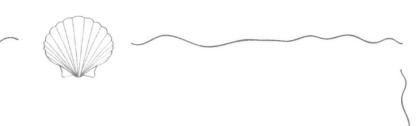

I send thee a shell from the ocean-beach;
But listen thou well, for my shell hath speech.
Hold to thine ear
And plain thou'lt hear
Tales of ships.

—Charles Henry Webb, *With a Nantucket Shell*

Date

Name

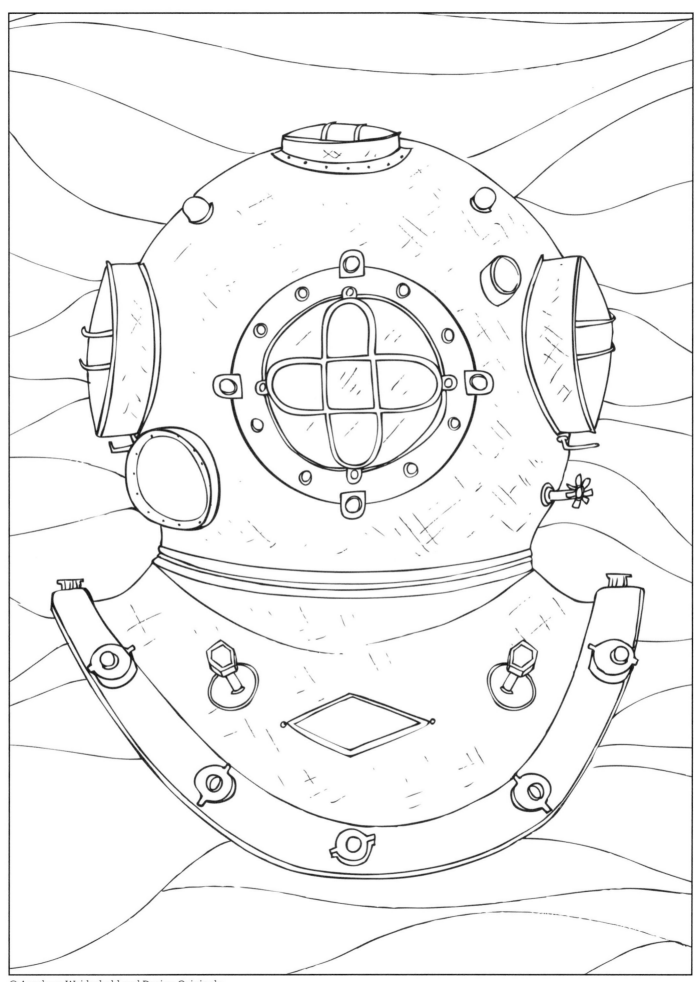

I need the sea because it teaches me.

—Pablo Neruda, *The Sea*

Date

Name

In order for the light to shine so brightly, the
darkness must also be present.

—Sir Francis Bacon

Date

Name

I wanted freedom, open air, and adventure.
I found it on the sea.

—Alain Gerbault

Date   Name

Smell the sea and feel the sky, let your soul
and spirit fly into the mystic.

—Van Morrison

Date

Name

I must go down to the sea again, to the lonely sea and the sky,
And all I ask is a tall ship and a star to steer her by.

—John Masefield, *Sea Fever*

Date   Name

 © Arrolynn Weiderhold and Design Originals

Complementary colors like orange and blue will really pop against one another. Some light research into color theory will help you gain confidence selecting colors.

The sea! the sea! the open sea!
The blue, the fresh, the ever free!

—Barry Cornwall, *The Sea*

For water, try a color scheme that uses different
shades of blue, green, and purple.

The waves of the sea help me get back to me.

—Unknown

© Arrolynn Weiderhold and Design Originals

Take inspiration from the real-world colors of the image
you are coloring. These pastel seashell shades create
a soft beachy color palette.

At the beach, life is different. Time doesn't move hour to hour, but mood to moment. We live by the currents, plan by the tides, and follow the sun.

—Sandy Gingras

Get playful with your color choices! Take inspiration from the fun patterns in this design and pair them with bright summery colors.

Life's roughest storms prove the strength
of our anchors.

—Unknown

Blue is a fitting color for this nautical design. Pair it with light, bright colors that will stand out against it.

We cannot direct the wind,
but we can adjust the sails.

—Unknown

WORK LIKE A CAPTAIN

PLAY LIKE A PIRATE

Try a different take on a classic nautical color scheme by using tints and shades of red, blue, brown, and gray.

I am the master of my fate,
I am the captain of my soul.

—William Ernest Henley, *Invictus*

Rich red and navy blue create a classic nautical-inspired color scheme.

Now, bring me that horizon.

—Captain Jack Sparrow,
Pirates of the Caribbean: The Curse of the Black Pearl

Take inspiration from the natural world and try a blue
and green color scheme for these sea turtles.

Live in the sunshine, swim the sea,
Drink the wild air's salubrity.

—Ralph Waldo Emerson, *Merlin's Song*

That the sea is one of the most beautiful and
magnificent sights in Nature, all admit.

—John Joly

Date   Name

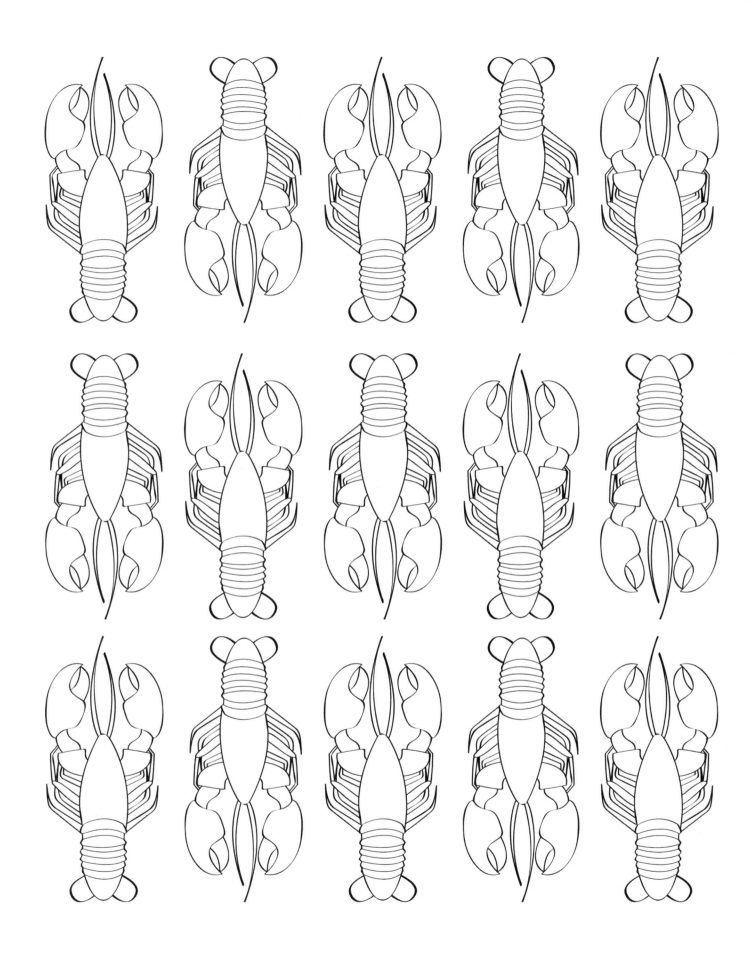

There is a pleasure in the pathless woods,
There is a rapture on the lonely shore,
There is society where none intrudes,
By the deep Sea, and music in its roar:
I love not Man the less, but Nature more.

—George Gordon Byron, *Childe Harold's Pilgrimage*

Date   Name

the OCEAN is CALLING

Heaven seems a little closer when
you are near the ocean.

—Unknown

Date   Name

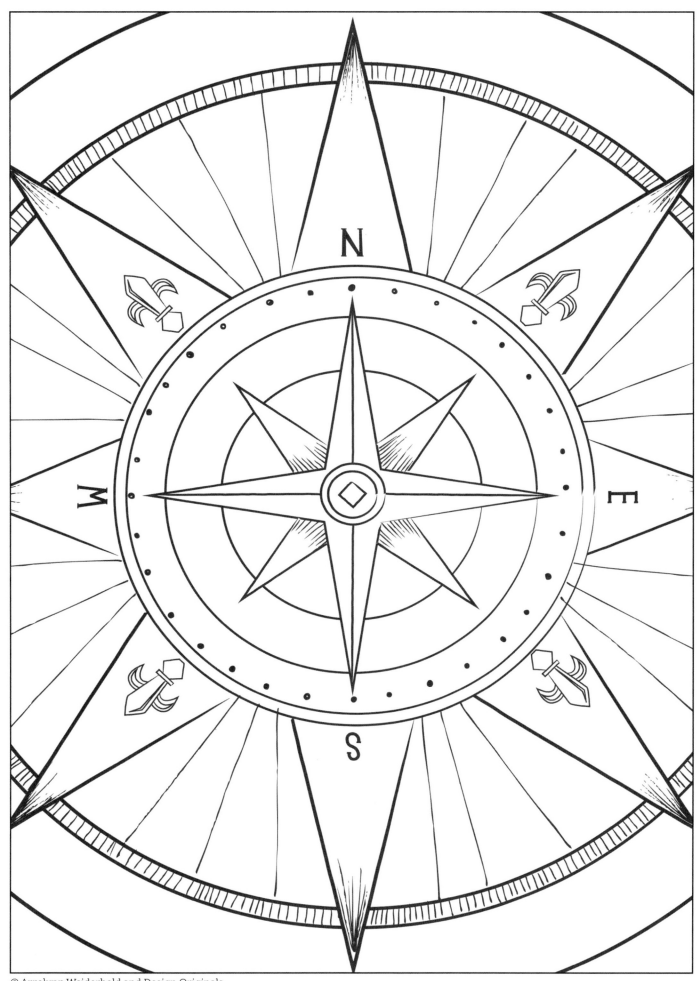

I am not afraid of storms for I am
learning how to sail my ship.

—Louisa May Alcott

Date   Name

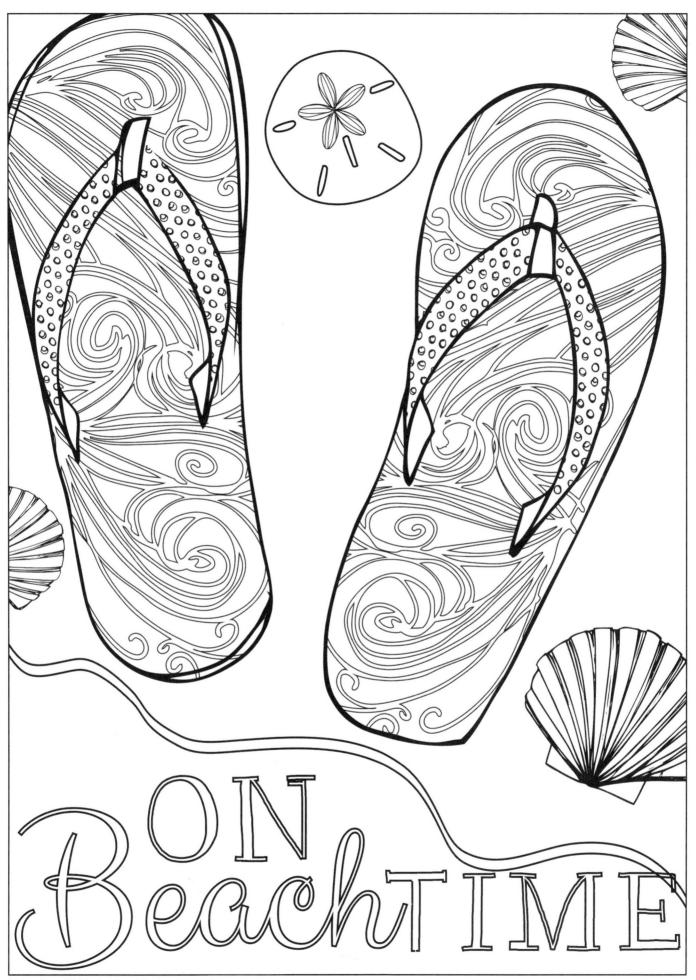

Everyone should believe in something.
I believe I should go to the beach.

—Unknown

Date   Name

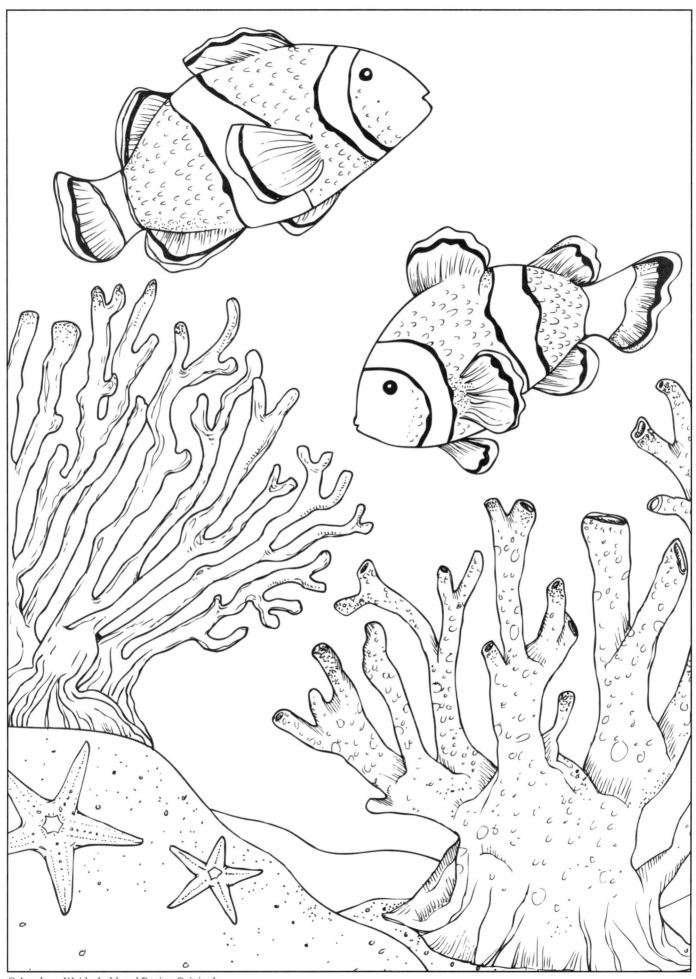

The heart of man is very much like the sea,
it has its storms, it has its tides, and in its
depths it has its pearls too.

—Vincent van Gogh

Date   Name

Waves are the voices of tides. Tides are life.

—Tamora Pierce, *Sandry's Book*

Date   Name

If my ship sails from sight, it doesn't mean my journey ends. It simply means the river bends.

—Enoch Powell

Date   Name

To unpathed waters, undreamed shores.

—William Shakespeare, *Winter's Tale*

Date   Name

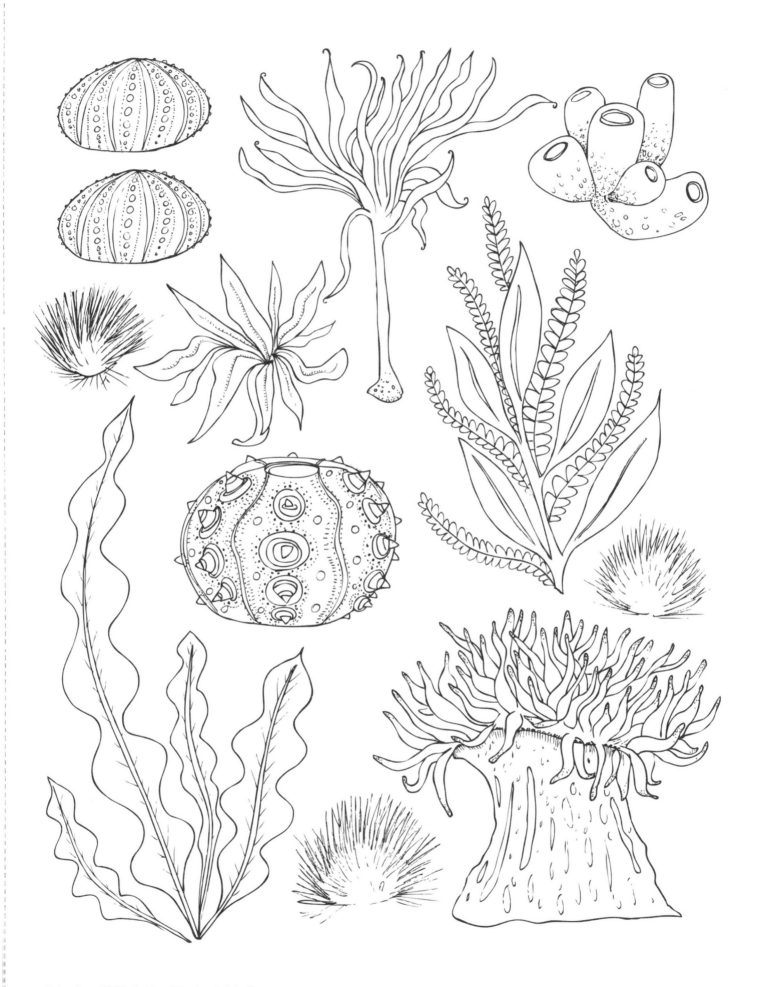

When a man comes to like a sea life,
he is not fit to live on land.

—Samuel Johnson

Date

Name

At night, when the sky is full of stars
and the sea is still you get the wonderful sensation
that you are floating in space.

—Natalie Wood

Date   Name

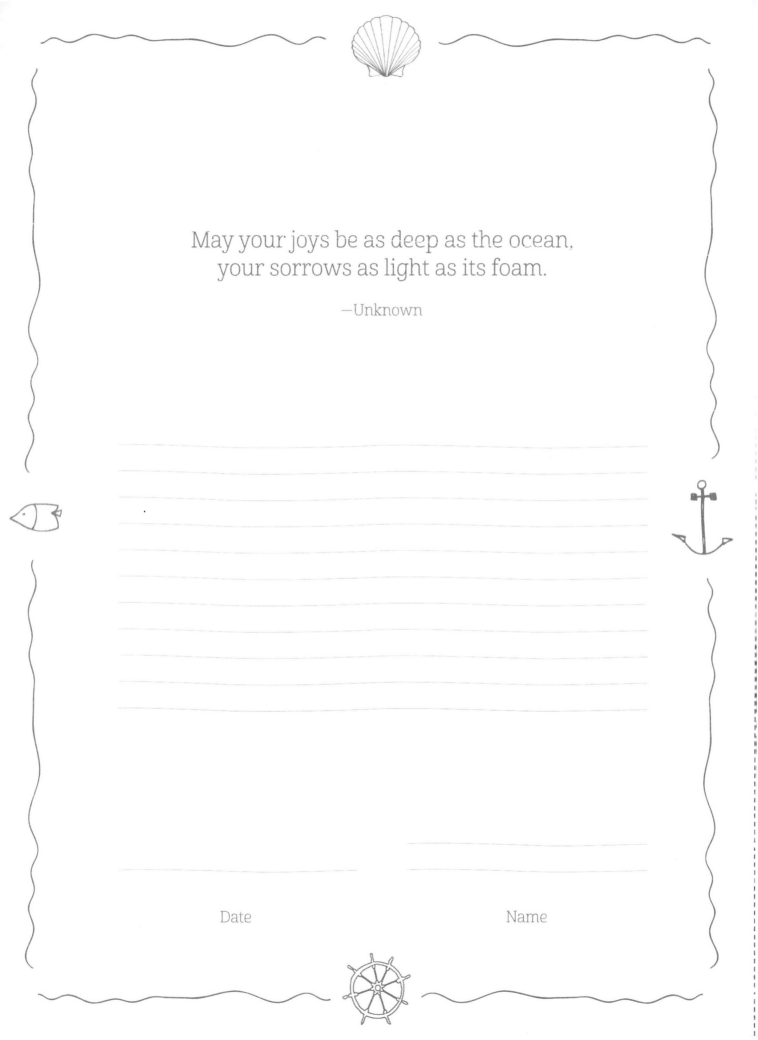

May your joys be as deep as the ocean,
your sorrows as light as its foam.

—Unknown

Date

Name

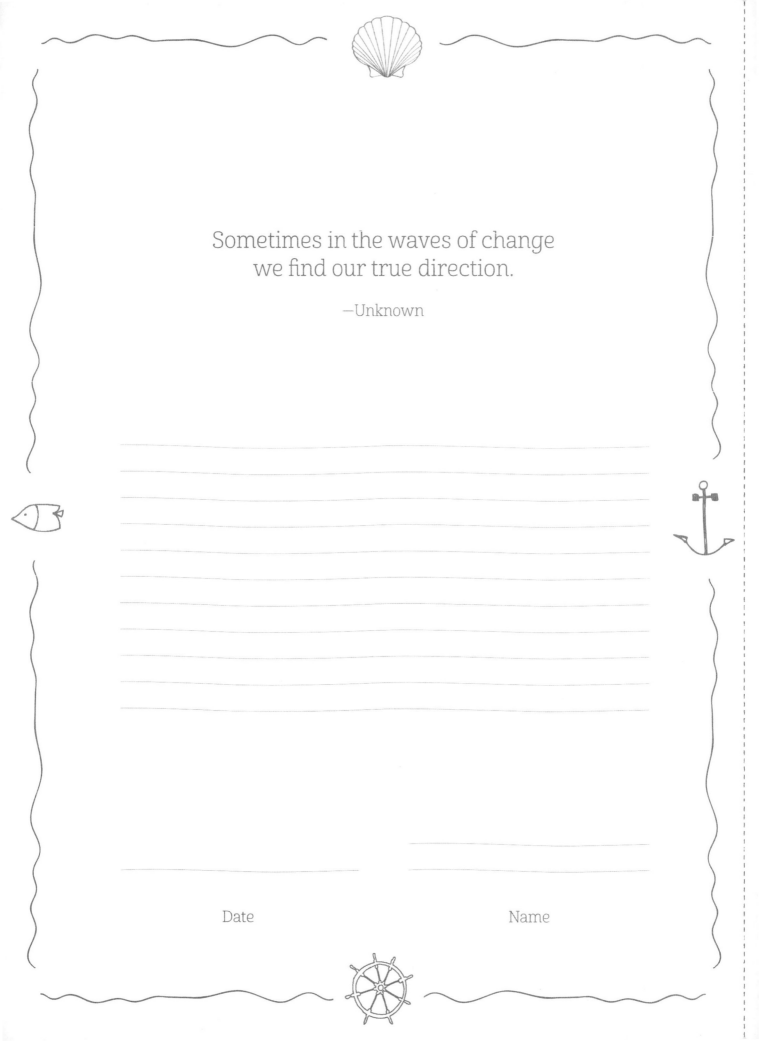

Sometimes in the waves of change
we find our true direction.

—Unknown

Date   Name

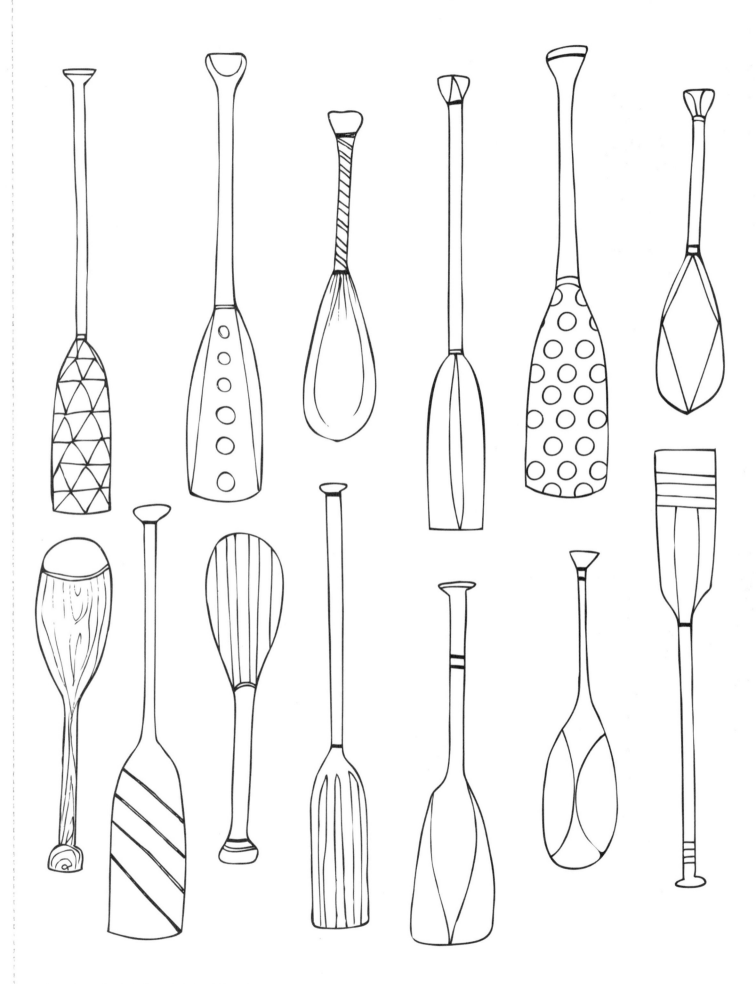

At sea, I learned how little a person needs,
not how much.

—Robin Lee Graham

Date   Name

You can never cross the ocean unless you have
the courage to lose sight of the shore.

—Unknown

_____

Date   Name

I think I love the rain because I am a mermaid
who lives too far from the ocean.

—Unknown

_____
_____
_____
_____
_____
_____
_____
_____
_____
_____
_____
_____

Date   Name

Eternity begins and ends with the ocean's tides.

—Unknown

Date   Name

Swim IN EVERY Ocean

If there is magic on this planet
it is contained in water.

—Loren Eiseley

Date   Name

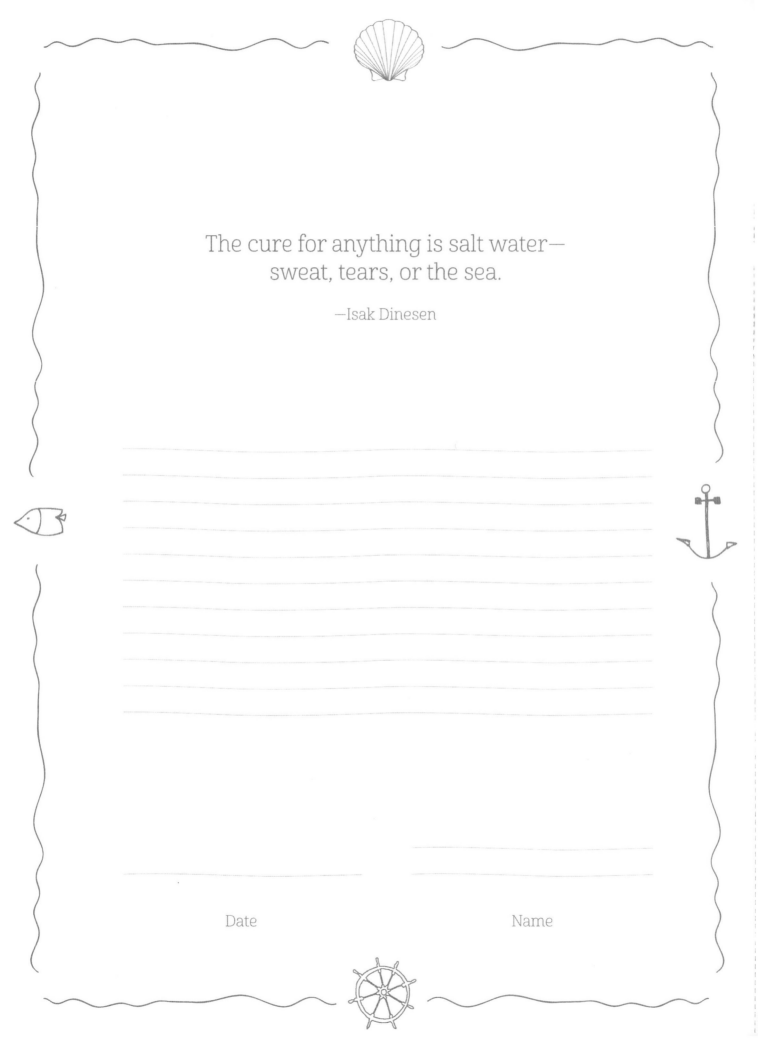

The cure for anything is salt water—
sweat, tears, or the sea.

—Isak Dinesen

Date

Name

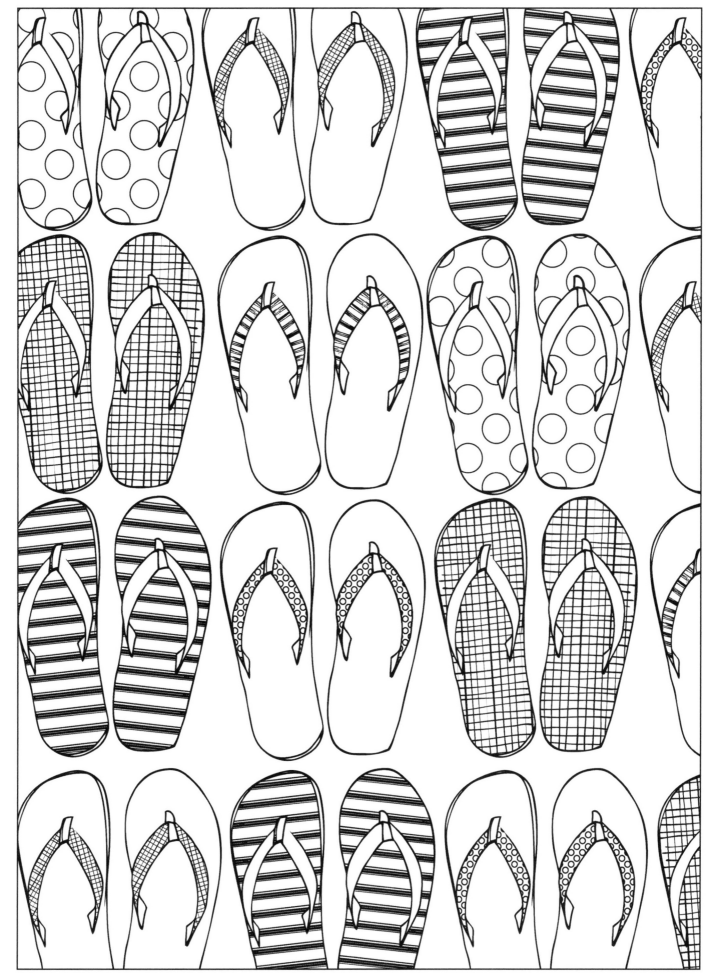

Once your feet have touched the warm
sun-drenched sand of the seashore you will
never ever be the same.

—Unknown

Date   Name

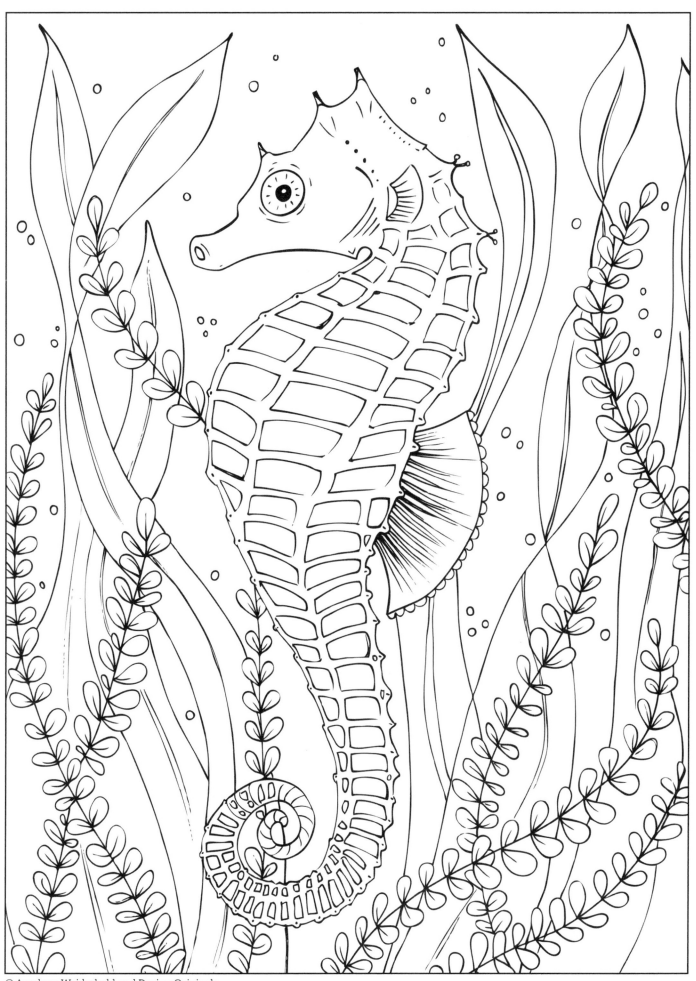

We are tied to the ocean. And when we go back to the sea, whether it is to sail or to watch—we are going back from whence we came.

—John F. Kennedy

Date

Name

If the ocean can calm itself, so can you.
We are both salt water mixed with air.

—Nayyirah Waheed

Date   Name

And never a ship sails out of the bay
But carries my heart as a stowaway!

—Roselle Mercier Montgomery, *The Stowaway*

Date

Name

The sea lives in every one of us.

—Wyland

Date   Name

You are not a drop in the ocean,
you are the entire ocean in a drop.

—Rumi

Date   Name

In every outthrust headland, in every curving beach, in every grain of sand there is the story of the earth.

—Rachel Carson

Date

Name

Our memories of the ocean will linger on, long after our footprints in the sand are gone.

—Unknown

Date

Name

The days pass happily with me
wherever my ship sails.

—Joshua Slocum

Date

Name

Turn your face to the sun and the shadows
will fall behind you.

—Maori proverb

_____

Date   Name

Till my soul is full of longing
For the secret of the sea,
And the heart of the great ocean
Sends a thrilling pulse through me.

—Henry Wadsworth Longfellow, *The Secret of the Sea*

Date

Name

For whatever we lose (like a you or a me),
It's always our self we find in the sea.

—e. e. cummings

Date

Name

Blue is known as a sad color, but when I see the ocean, all my sorrow is washed away.

—Unknown

Date

Name